HILLSBOROUGH
An Illustrated History and Companion

Paintings by
Alison Brown

Historical text by
Simon Walker

First published by Cottage Publications,
Donaghadee N. Ireland 1994.

Printed in Singapore

ISBN 0 9516402 5 9

List of Contents

The Artist

Born in Portadown, Alison has lived in Co. Down since she was four years old. She now resides near Donaghadee with her husband, Tim and daughters, Ruth, Clare and Rachel.

Alison's preferred medium is watercolour in which she delicately captures the character of older buildings which are her favourite subject. She has successfully exhibited in numerous exhibitions and has twice been a prizewinner in the much respected Percy French Watercolour Competition.

In recent years, Alison and Tim have established a small publishing company, 'Cottage Publications'. This is the fourth book in their 'Illustrated History and Companion' series illustrated by Alison.

The Author

Simon Walker is a native of Hillsborough, where his family has lived for generations and were once members of the Hillsborough Guard. He graduated from Queen's University, Belfast with a degree in Modern History although he also studied ancient history and archaeology.

As well as his special interest in local history, Simon is involved in keeping alive Hillsborough's tradition of church bell-ringing and is the conductor of the local ringing society. He has written several articles for local and national magazines on both subjects.

Hillsborough:—
Of Hills and Glen

The village of Hillsborough is renowned for its picturesque architecture and delightful 'olde worlde' charm. Compared with other towns and villages throughout the country Hillsborough has retained many more of its older buildings giving residents and visitors alike a sense of long and distinguished history behind every street and building in the town.

Given this initial impression it is perhaps surprising that Hillsborough's rise to prominence really only starts in the early 17th Century. Like much of Ireland at that time the area was heavily wooded and the countryside was dotted with raths. These raised circular rings of earth enclosed by rough wooden fences, housed much of the native population who lived under the rule of local chieftains. One of these ancient farmsteads, 'Fox Fort', can still be seen in the Forest Park. The largest settlement in the area was located where Hillsborough Fort now stands and was the home of the Magennes Clan who ruled large tracts of land in County Down and controlled the important road from Dublin to the northern ports such as Carrickfergus. The place was known as 'Cromlyn', from the Irish 'Crolm ghlinn', which means 'the crooked glen' and refers to the twisting stream which still meanders through the area where the little cluster of dwellings was situated.

However, an indication of the hamlet's insignificance can be seen by the fact that when the Normans came they built a motte and bailey castle a few miles to the north at Duneight and one to the south, at Dromore, whilst Cromlyn was by-passed by any such developments.

While there is little clear historical record of the area before the early 1600's it is thought that there was an ecclesiastical foundation around 600 AD although the earliest physical evidence of Christian worship is the ruined twelfth century Chapel of Cromlyn. It was dedicated to the Irish saint, Malachi O'Morgair, who had been Bishop of Down and Archbishop of Armagh and who died in 1148 whilst visiting St. Bernard of Clairveux at his home in France. In 1622 a survey by the Church of Ireland, 'the Ulster Visitation', noted that Cromlyn Chapel was in ruins and there was no fit place to worship.

A change in the fortunes of Cromlyn came about as a result of unrest in Ireland. In 1593 the Irish Earls, under Hugh O'Neill, rose against Queen Elizabeth I, forcing her to send an army to Ireland to restore order. The army was led by Walter Devereux, Earl of Essex, who had under his command an officer named Sir Moyses Hill. When peace was secured Sir Moyses took an Irish wife and, as the English were on the ascent and the Irish Lords were in decline, he began to buy land in Ireland. By the time of his death in 1630 at his fortified residence at Hill Hall near Lisburn (from which the village of Hillhall gets its name), he had accumulated large tracts of land in Antrim and Down. This included 5204 acres around the Cromlyn area acquired from Bryan McCrory Magennes in 1611. Over the next three hundred years the

Hill family would use this land and their wealth to shape virtually every facet of the development of Hillsborough.

The first steps in this direction were taken by Sir Moyses' son, Peter Hill, who laid the foundations for what we now know as Hillsborough. In 1630 he built the Fort to protect the main road between Carrickfergus and Dublin. He also began laying out a village and in 1636 built a church near the old Cromlyn Chapel. This church, and much of the village, was destroyed in the rebellion of 1641 when the native Irish rose in rebellion against the incoming settlers in many parts of Ireland.

As Peter died childless, his brother, Colonel Arthur Hill, inherited the estate in 1655 and set about repairing the damage caused by the rebellion. In 1662 he built a new church 'dedicated to St. Malachias', following the tradition of the saintly dedication of the chapel of Cromlyn. The church was consecrated by his friend, Bishop Jeremy Taylor who had been a chaplain to King Charles I and had married the King's illegitimate daughter, Joanna. Despite the fact that this made him King Charles II's brother in law the marriage hampered Taylor's promotion in the church because the new King did not want the public to be constantly reminded of an extra marital affair which would tarnish the memory of his otherwise saintly father. As such an Irish Bishopric was considered sufficiently out of the public eye to avoid any embarrassment. Both Bishop Taylor and his wife, technically a full member of the Royal Family, are buried in Dromore Cathedral.

Colonel Arthur remodelled the Fort and was granted a charter making him 'Hereditary Constable of Hillsborough Fort' with the command of twenty warders, or 'Castlemen'.

Today there is still a bugler employed to keep this tradition alive. The uniform of the warders consists of a red tunic, white breeches and a black cockade hat with a white plume. The bugler has the added embellishment of epaulettes. Until the end of the last century the warders were armed with muskets, but these were reduced to curved swords.

By 1662 the old name of Cromlyn had ceased to be used altogether, for in this year a Royal Charter made the town into a borough – Hillsborough. The charter gave Hillsborough the right to send two representatives to the Irish Parliament in Dublin, and to have a Town Corporation. While these initial steps towards democracy were welcomed, it is interesting to note that until these parliamentary seats were abolished by the Act of Union some one hundred and forty years later, one of the elected representatives always happened to be a member of the Hill family! The Corporation consisted of a Sovereign and twelve Burgesses, as well as a Recorder and a Sergeant to carry the mace. The mace would have been displayed while the Corporation was conducting business, and was placed on their pew in the parish church. The original silver mace was made in 1674 and is now kept in the Ulster Museum. A new, larger mace was presented by the First Marquis of Downshire and it can still be seen on the Corporation pew every Sunday. It was made in London by Charles Aldridge in 1786.

The new-found importance of Hillsborough was underlined in 1690 when King William III stayed at the Fort for four days on his way to the Battle of the Boyne. Before leaving, the King made a grant of money, known as the 'Regium Donum' to the Irish Presbyterian clergy for their loyalty. A stone tablet at the entrance gate of the Fort commemorates this event.

Recognition by the Crown of the importance of the Hill family came in 1717 when Trevor Hill was made Viscount Hillsborough by King George I. He was succeeded by his son, Wills Hill, in whose lifetime Hillsborough acquired the appearance it retains to this day. Walter Harris, in his book, "The Ancient and Present State of County Down", written in 1744, tells us of Wills Hill's intention to rebuild and improve the town. He says, "The present Right Honourable Lord intends to build a new Mansion House, and has fixed on a plan for a new Town to be built in the form of a large Square, with a stately Market House in the Centre: to settle in which great Encouragement will be given to Linen Manufacturers."

As well as implementing these grand plans in the locality Wills was also a figure of international importance due to the high offices he held in politics. He was the Secretary of State for America during the time of the struggle for independence and it was this which occasioned the visit of Benjamin Franklin to Hillsborough in January 1772. It is clear from the records that Franklin and Wills Hill did not like each other which, coupled with the fact that King George III felt that his American secretary was "amiable, but the least man of business", cannot have helped an already difficult situation. In fact, throughout the rest of his reign the King blamed Wills Hill personally for the loss of America. However, amongst other achievements, Wills sponsored the publication of Goldsmith's 'The Deserted Village' and invented the screw-on top for lemonade bottles! He was created Earl of Hillsborough in 1751 and first Marquis of Downshire in 1789.

In his rebuilding of the town, Wills began by restoring the Fort which had lain derelict for a number of years. He reconstructed the gatehouse in the 'Gothick' style and built a church-like gazebo on the north wall. Behind the Fort was an avenue of trees leading to the Hill residence which stood where the park lake now is. Writing in her diary in 1758, Mrs Delany, wife of the Dean of Down who travelled widely and observed the lives of the gentry in 18th century, noted the work which was being carried out and that the area within the walls of the Fort was being used as a menagerie.

It was part of Wills' plan to build a new house (the present Hillsborough Castle) and give the old one to the Bishop of Down. This bears out the fact that he hoped the parish church would become a cathedral to replace the ruined one at Downpatrick which had been destroyed in the 16th century on the orders of the Lord Deputy of Ireland, Leonard Grey. Between 1760 and 1772, Wills spent in the region of £20,000 on the restoration and rebuilding of the church. It is not known who the architect was, but it is clear that a large contributor to the design was the Earl of Hillsborough himself. Provision was made for the building to become a cathedral and a beautiful throne for the bishop was built, but was never used as such because the church authorities wanted Downpatrick to retain its ecclesiastical dignity. The Sanctuary was lined with cedar from the Lebanon, prompted by the biblical description of Solomon's Temple, whilst the East Window was based an a design by Sir Joshua Reynolds. The organ in the west gallery was built by John Snetzler, a native of Bavaria who lived in England because he preferred English beer to German beer! A bed of daffodils in the shape of a star outside the front door is said to mark the spot where a steeplejack met his death by falling from the spire during building work. However, there is no record of this having happened as Wills Hill kept a detailed account of all construction work on the church and he makes no mention of such an incident. A ring of bells was provided for the church, one of which is was inscribed "Prosperity to the town". This was exactly what Wills had in mind for Hillsborough.

Wills was keen to provide employment for his tenants. In 1760 he had the Market House built in the Square to act as the centre of the local linen trade with a shambles (a yard and pens for cattle) nearby. Between 1750 and 1780 many of the houses which line the streets today were constructed. Hillsborough Castle was begun about 1758, but was only completed during the lifetime of the second Marquis of Downshire by the architect, R. P. Brettingham.

An indication of the growing unrest in Ireland at that time can be seen in an incident which took place in Hillsborough on 16th October 1795. The Marquis of Downshire's agent records "a serious affray in the market. The Kilwarlin boys were the leaders... Four were lodged in the Black Hole but escaped... I got through Lord Doneraile a sergeant's guard from the camp (the Tholsel being threatened) and the sovereign accompanied me to every public house and forbid the sale of liquor." We cannot say for certain where the 'black-hole' was, but it was most likely in the vicinity of the Fort.

When the United Irishmen rose in 1798, Hillsborough seems to have avoided the very worst of the trouble, although a number of people were hanged on the church gates. A group of rebels stole some arms from the Fort, but this was a very mild incident compared to the trouble which occurred elsewhere in County Down.

By the time the third Marquis came of age in 1809, the Downshire estate was amongst the largest in Ireland, with, it is claimed, 100,000 tenants. Large celebrations held at the Fort were frequent at this time, but the most spectacular of all must have been the party for the marriage of the future fourth Marquis in 1837. A poem of fifteen verses was written to describe the occasion, one of which reads:

> "In the rear of the fortress the tables were spread,
> With roast beef and mutton, plum pudding and bread,
> And three thousand five hundred to dinner sat down,
> A magnificent party for Hillsborough town"

Local folklore maintains that thirteen people died as a result of the vast intake of food and drink!

The respect and affection in which the third and fourth Marquises were held is evidenced by their monuments, erected by their tenants. The granite column on a hilltop on the Dromore Road commemorates the third Marquis who died in 1845. It was placed here in 1848 and it was claimed that all the land which could be seen from the top was owned by the Downshire estate. The fourth Marquis is remembered by his bronze statue the 'Black Man' opposite the church gates. He was known as the 'Big Marquis' and the statue conveys his impressive build.

The fourth Marquis was involved in a very unfortunate incident when he was an undergraduate at Oxford University. During a light-hearted scuffle he had struck Lord Conyers Osborne, a fellow student, on the head and killed him. When the matter was investigated it was found that Lord Osborne suffered from an aneurysm and could have died at any moment and the death was put down to 'chance medley'. Even if his youth was blighted by such tragedy, the fourth Marquis was to earn respect for his supportive stance to his tenants during the potato famine, donating more than £20,000 of his own money for relief.

The fifth Marquis succeeded his father in 1868, but died six years later, aged only 29. It is an ironic coincidence that when the church bells were being tolled for the fifth Marquis' funeral, the fifth bell cracked. The estate passed to the sixth Marquis in 1874 when he was still an infant, and his affairs were managed by his uncle, Lord Arthur Hill.

Lord Arthur's first wife had died within a year of their marriage, but the events surrounding his second marriage bring a touch of romance to our local history. He fell in love with a lady named Annie Harrison who was staying in Hillsborough, but his family felt that she was not from sufficiently wealthy stock. On learning of this, Miss Harrison left and all Lord Arthur's attempts to contact her failed. Sadly, he resigned himself to the fact that he would not see her again. One night while visiting the theatre in London, Lord Arthur was very moved by the words of a song. The song began thus:

"In the gloaming, oh my darling,
Think not bitterly of me,
Though I stole away in silence,
Left you lonely, set you free.
It was best to leave you thus, dear,
Best for you and best for me".

When Lord Arthur enquired about the name of the composer, he discovered that it was Annie Harrison! So, they were reunited and decided to marry and, as in all good stories, they lived happily ever after.

Keeping music in mind, we note that in 1878 one William Harty was appointed organist of the parish church. Before moving into the Organist's House in Ballynahinch Street the Harty family lived briefly in Main Street. It was here that his son, Hamilton Harty, was born. Young Hamilton often accompanied his father to have lessons on the church organ for, like his eight brothers and sisters, he was very musical. Hamilton was indeed exceptional and was to pursue a remarkable career. Moving to London he became a conductor and composer of note. In 1920 he reached the pinnacle of his career by being appointed conductor of the Halle Orchestra. In 1925 he received a knighthood. His compositions include works with an Irish flavour, 'The Irish Symphony' and 'The Children of Lir'. He is well known for his orchestration of Handel's 'Water Music'. Sir Hamilton Harty died in 1941 and his ashes were placed under a limestone birdbath outside the door of Hillsborough Parish Church. The birdbath is the work of Rosamund Praeger and depicts musicians playing traditional instruments around the base.

Further alterations were made to the Castle in the late 1820's by Thomas Duff, and again a few years later by William Sands but by around 1800 the town stood very much as we see it today except that it had an extra street. Moira Street, which no longer exists, ran from the south side of the Market House right past the windows of Hillsborough Castle. Some people even claimed that, from the street, they had seen the Marquis of Downshire and his family having their breakfast! Moira Street was demolished when the new Moira Road was created in 1826. Debate exists as to the date of the new road, as the old Moira Street can still be seen on an Ordnance Survey map of 1833. However, it is probable that work on the new road did commence in 1826 but was still incomplete seven years later, given that it involved substantially raising the ground level on the Dromore Road at the Square.

In the Square was the Royal Corporation Arms Hotel, an imposing Georgian building which was burnt down as recently as 1943. In 1800 a brewery was built opposite the church gates. This was a gothic building to match the church. Although the brewery was demolished in the nineteenth century, the cellars remained hidden until they were discovered over fifty years ago during work on the road. At the foot of the hill where the public toilets now stand was a beautiful stone built three storey house with a fanlight above the door. This closed off the end of the entrance to the church, but was pulled down and replaced with the incongruous toilets. With the exception of these buildings, the Georgian town of Hillsborough remains intact.

During the halcyon days after the opening of the Lagan Canal in 1794 there were great hopes that this new transport system would bring great prosperity to the area and Lisburn Street was called 'Great Newport Street'. Unfortunately, though its construction had cost £70,000, the canal was poorly designed and underfunded. It never reached its potential and with the arrival of the railway in 1863 (with a station at the Lisburn end of Culcavey Road) the little remaining trade on the canal disappeared and it fell into total disrepair.

Other street names have also changed over the years. Main Street was once known as 'Castle Street', whilst Ballynahinch Street was, at first, called 'New Street', a name later given to the present Arthur Street. Behind the Square is Barrack Court or Inn Court. The two names for this little enclave remind us that there was a barrack nearby in Moira Street, and that the village once had a hotel at its centre.

By the beginning of the twentieth century the Hill family were spending less time in Hillsborough, although they maintained a deep interest in the affairs of the place. After 1913 Hillsborough Castle was leased out, and Sir Thomas Dixon lived there for a time.

The Castle was sold to the Northern Ireland Government in 1924 for use as the residence of the Governor and since that time the name of Hillsborough has been associated with most major events in the history of Northern Ireland. Over the next fifty years Government House, as the Castle was styled, saw many important visitors come and go, among them members of the Royal Family, including the Queen on numerous occasions. Five Governors lived here before the post was abolished with the demise of the Northern Ireland Government in 1973. Since then the house is once more officially called Hillsborough Castle. The Secretary of State for Northern Ireland stays here and it is still the scene of many important events.

Today Hillsborough is a popular place to live and the last twenty years have witnessed development around the town on a large scale. Offsetting this loss of surrounding countryside has been the greater attention paid to the upkeep of the historic and attractive buildings in the centre of the town which still exudes a charm and elegance found in few other places in this country.

Formal recognition of the value of the town came in 1976 when Hillsborough was declared a 'Conservation Area'. As cars speed up and down our streets and bulldozers open the earth to make way for more new houses it may seem a far cry from the desolate hamlet of Cromlyn which four hundred years ago seemed destined to remain in obscurity forever. However, the same little stream twists its way through the 'crooked glen', past the ruins of the old chapel, just as it has done for centuries. Even in the midst of change some things remain constant.

Major Events in Hillsborough's History

c.600 A.D.	Ecclesiastical settlement in the area.
1148	St. Malachi, Archbishop of Armagh and Bishop of Down, dies while visiting St. Bernard of Clairveux.
1170	The Normans come to Ireland. A motte and bailey castle is built at Duneight, three miles from the hamlet of Cromlyn.
1593	Seven Years War. Elizabeth I sends an army to Ireland under the Earl of Essex. Sir Moyses Hill is amongst the officers.
1611	Moyses Hill buys over 5000 acres from the Magennes family.
1630	Peter Hill starts building the Fort.
1636	The first parish church is built.
1641	The Irish Rebellion. The church is burnt down and the Fort damaged.
1650	Colonel Arthur Hill repairs the Fort.
1660	Charles II grants a Royal Charter to the town, making it a borough and giving it the right to send two representatives to the Parliament in Dublin.
1662	St. Malachi's Parish Church is built by Colonel Arthur Hill.
1690	King William III stays at the Fort for four days on his way to the Boyne. He grants the Regium Donum to the Presbyterian clergy.
1744	The antiquarian, Walter Harris, visits the town and describes it in his book, "The Ancient and Present State of County Down".
1758	Wills Hill, Earl of Hillsborough, reconstructs the gatehouse of the Fort.

1760	Work of restoration and rebuilding of the parish church commences. The Market House is built.
1760-80	The town is laid out as we see it today.
1772	Benjamin Franklin visits Hillsborough.
1773	The church is reopened.
1789	Wills Hill is created first Marquis of Downshire.
1793	Wills Hill dies, aged 76.
1798	Skirmishes in Hillsborough as part of the United Irishmen rising.
1826	The grounds of Hillsborough Castle are enclosed and the Dublin Road constructed.
1833	The Presbyterian Church is built.
1848	The Downshire Column is erected.
1863	The Banbridge, Lisburn and Belfast Railway is opened, with a station at Hillsborough.
1879	Sir Hamilton Harty is born in a house in Main Street.
1924	The seventh Marquis of Downshire sells Hillsborough Castle to the new Government of Northern Ireland for use as the official residence of the Governor.
1936	Hillsborough Castle is damaged by fire.
1943	Royal Corporation Arms Hotel destroyed by fire.
1964	Council offices built on the site of the hotel.
1973	Northern Ireland Government suspended, and the post of Governor ceases to exist.
1974	Belfast to Newry By-pass opened.
1976	Hillsborough is declared a 'Conservation Area'.
1985	Anglo-Irish Agreement signed in Hillsborough Castle.

Alison Brown 1994.

Name and Address	*Telephone*

Harty House, Ballynahinch Street

This was the residence for the organist of the parish church, and was built incorporating the remnants of a much older house. From the garden the organist was able to walk along a path, through a park called 'the Pleasure Ground', and into the church grounds through a curious little gateway. From 1878 to 1918 the organist was William Harty, whose son, Hamilton, became a famous composer and conductor. From early music lessons in this house and on the church organ, Hamilton Harty rose to the post of conductor of the Halle Orchestra.

With Thanks to G & H Bell Ltd.

B

Name and Address	*Telephone*

The Market House

When the Hills laid out the town they wished to promote local trade and commerce. In this part of Co. Down the linen trade was extremely important and the Market House was built in 1760 to act as a centre for local weavers to come and sell their produce. However market day was not exclusively for linen but also for the sale of livestock as evidenced by the nearby shambles. The Market House was extended in 1810 when a new clock and bell were installed. Until the last war the curfew was rung on the bell every evening. With the demise of the linen trade the building was used as a joiner's shop, the Downshire estate office and latterly, a courthouse.

With Thanks to The Chatham Chest Gallery

STOP
Alison Brown 1994.

Name and Address	*Telephone*

St. Colman's, Reilly's Trench

Outside the village stands the simple Roman Catholic Church of St. Colman. The name Reilly's Trench perhaps came from a seventeenth century Royalist officer. There may have been a place of worship here since that time as a chapel 'of considerable antiquity' was burnt down by Royalists some time between 1742 and 1745. After this services were held in the open air, which was quite common during the penal era when non Anglicans (including among others, both Presbyterians and Roman Catholics) were not allowed to have their churches within the town boundary. The present church was built in 1805 on land given by the Marquis of Downshire.

Alison Brown 1994.

Name and Address	*Telephone*

COWDY CRAFTS, 20 MAIN STREET

No. 20 is one of a group of three houses sharing many architectural details in their basic structure. On a map drawn by John Webb in 1810 these houses are not shown and as such they must have been amongst the last to be built in Main Street sometime early in the 19th Century. The present owner, Patrick Cowdy, has been in business in Hillsborough for many years specialising in high quality crafts and giftware including a number of lines relating directly to the town. His shop is well known by locals and visitors alike and is typical of the elegant traditional shops which can be found in Hillsborough.

With Thanks to P. R. Cowdy Crafts

Alison Brown 1994

Name and Address	*Telephone*

The Quaker Church

The village's Quaker congregation fled from England in the eighteenth century to avoid persecution. Their first church stood on Barrack Hill, a street which was demolished in the early nineteenth century. At this time the present church was built. The original 'Sleeping Place', (graveyard) was close to the old church and was enclosed within the grounds of Hillsborough Castle in 1826 although the Quaker church retains rights of access to look after the burial ground. Originally their entrance was through the 'Quaker Gate' which is on the Dromore Road opposite Park Street.

Alison Brown 1994

Name and Address	*Telephone*

Fourth Marquis of Downshire Statue

The statue of Arthur, fourth Marquis of Downshire, is the work of Samuel Ferres Lynn and was erected in 1868. This Lord Downshire was known as the 'Big Marquis' and the statue conveys his impressive stature. During the Potato Famine he was one of the few landlords who stayed in Ireland and he gave £20,000 of his own money for the relief of the starving. The surrounding garden was once the site of a brewery, which was a gothic-style building to match the church opposite.

With Thanks to V. E. Reaney Chemist

Alison Brown 1994

Name and Address	*Telephone*

The Square

This imposing red brick house and the houses next to it were built by Wills Hill in 1780 at the time when the Square took its present form. These houses were designed in the manner of Town Houses in Dublin and London and, although on a smaller scale, were for the more affluent tenants who could afford to live close to Hillsborough Castle and therefore to the Downshire family. In the last century Lord Arthur Hill had a desire to name many of the more important houses in the Square after his Downshire ancestors, and so we have Hill House, Blundell House and Trevor House.

With Thanks to The Old Coach House

Alison Brown 1994

Name and Address	*Telephone*

THE SHAMBLES

In the nineteenth century a livestock fair was held in Hillsborough on the third Wednesday in February, May, August and November. A shambles for penning cattle had been built by the first Marquis of Downshire near the old Rectory on the Dublin Road. When the level of the road was raised in 1826 the existing shambles was created. There is still a weighbridge for the animals dating from this period in the courtyard of the present complex. In 1970 the building was converted into a local art centre.

With Thanks to Bowers Auctions

Alison Brown 1994

I

Name and Address	*Telephone*

NORTHERN BANK, BALLYNAHINCH STREET

Blessington House was built by the first Marquis of Downshire to provide a residence for his agent. The importance of Blessington House was emphasised by the imposing doric portico and beautiful lamp-standards. It is shocking to think that at one stage the third Marquis considered demolishing this building to alter the course of the street. Just before the turn of the century the residence of the agent was moved to Kilwarlin House at the end of Lisburn Street. Part of Blessington House was converted to a branch of the Northern Bank, although the pleasant facade of the house has been retained. Until the 1970's the bank manager actually lived in the building.

With Thanks to Northern Bank Limited

Alison Brown 1994.

Name and Address	*Telephone*

Downshire Monument

The handsome granite column on a hilltop just outside the town commemorates Arthur, third Marquis of Downshire who died in 1845 at his estate at Blessington, County Wicklow. The cause of death was reported as being a fall from his horse during a fit, although there were local rumours that he had been shot by one of his restless tenants. His funeral procession from Blessington to Hillsborough is said to have been the largest ever seen in Ireland. The column itself was paid for by the Marquis' tenants and friends and it is said that he owned all the land which could be seen from the top. The original plan to have four stone lions at the base was never carried out.

With Thanks to John Preston & Co (Belfast) Ltd.

Alison Brown 1994

Name and Address	*Telephone*

The Moravian Church

Situated about $1^1/_2$ miles outside the town is the Moravian Church with its manse and church hall. There has been a church here since 1754. The present church was built in 1834 by Basil Patras Zula, a Greek prince who had come to Ireland at the time of the Greek War of Independence. He had married an Irishwoman and under her guidance became a Moravian clergyman. So fearful was he of his disgruntled countrymen following him that he laid out the grounds of his church like a battlefield, with a high mound surrounded by a moat, whilst the manse had escape doors and a secret hide. Today the church is cared for by a devoted congregation.

Alison Brown 1994

Name and Address	*Telephone*

LISBURN STREET

This is the oldest part of the town and old photographs show the houses with whitewash over their stone walls. The street was, for a time in the last century, known as 'Great Newport Street'. Little alleys ran off at right angles, one of which was called 'Squeezegut Entry'. The Marquis of Downshire Tavern has been in operation since the eighteenth century and was even mentioned in a Georgian travelling directory. An old uniform of a Fort Warder is on display inside.

With Thanks to Down Decorators

Alison Brown 1994

Name and Address	*Telephone*

The Fort

In the troubled seventeenth century this was a strategic point on the main road between Carrickfergus and Dublin and the need to protect it was realised by Peter Hill who built the Fort in 1630. Further construction was carried out by Colonel Arthur Hill, who was made Constable of the Fort by King Charles II, with command of an army of twenty men, the Hillsborough Guard or 'Castlemen' as they were known locally. King William III stayed here on his way to the Boyne. After a period of relative peace in Ireland the place fell into disrepair, but in 1758 Wills Hill rebuilt the gatehouse in the gothic style and provided a pretty gazebo on the north wall. The Fort has been in state care since 1959.

With Thanks to Johnson's Coffee

HILLSIDE
Alison Brown 1994

Mc

Name and Address	*Telephone*

The Hillside, 21 Main Street

As the sign outside states, this has been a public house since 1777. Since the building dates from around that time this must have been the purpose for which it was built and doubtless in its time it would have served beer from the brewery which used to stand at the bottom of the street. The Hillside is a favourite stopping off place for visitors and locals alike and it maintains a fine reputation and has won many awards such as 'Pub of the Year'. Old photographs, taken at the turn of the century, show that the Hillside and the buildings next to it had stone frontages at that time.

With Thanks to The Hillside

Alison Brown 1994

Name and Address	*Telephone*

The Presbyterian Church

While the Penal Laws (which disadvantaged those who did not adhere to the Anglican Church) were applied, the local Presbyterians worshiped in a barn outside Hillsborough in the townland of Listullycurran. However something of a seachange in Presbyterian fortunes had taken place in Hillsborough when King William III granted the 'Regium Donum' or 'King's Money' to the Irish Presbyterian clergy in recognition of their loyalty. The first Presbyterian Church on the Lisburn Street site was built in 1833 on land given by the Marquis of Downshire. During its construction the congregation worshiped in the Market House. The church was completely rebuilt in 1885 and extended in 1959.

David
Graham
OPEN
Alison Brown
1994

Name and Address	*Telephone*

DAVID GRAHAM STUDIO, 14 MAIN STREET

One of a closely matched pair, No.14, like most houses in Main Street, was built by the first Marquis of Downshire. The real claim to fame of this house is that it was the birth-place of the famous composer and conductor, Sir Hamilton Harty. His father William became the organist of the Parish Church in 1878 but was still living in No.14 Main Street by the time Hamilton was born in 1879. The family did move shortly afterwards and it is the house in Ballynahinch Street which is more readily associated with Hamilton Harty. Today No.14 continues its artistic tradition, though in a somewhat more modern guise, as the David Graham Studio.

With Thanks to The David Graham Studio

Alison Brown 1994

Name and Address	*Telephone*

HILLSBOROUGH CASTLE

There seems to have been a house on this site since before 1758, when it was enlarged by the first Marquis of Downshire to replace his mansion in the present forest park. The enlargements were completed in 1797 four years after the death of the first Marquis. Further alterations took place between the late 1820's and 1840's, leaving the building much as we see it today. The Downshire family sold the castle to the Northern Ireland Government in 1924 and it became the residence of the Governor of Northern Ireland. From then until the suspension of the Stormont Parliament it was known as 'Government House' and has since been used by the Secretary of State.

With Thanks to The Outdoor Clothing Company

Alison Brown 1994

Name and Address	*Telephone*

NUMBER 5, MAIN STREET

This red brick house was obviously built at the same time as the house next door although through the years they have fulfiled very different functions. Until the start of this century next door (No. 7) was the police station and the basement still shows signs of being a cell. The two houses were probably built on the walls of older seventeenth century houses as the building material changes from brick to stone beneath the level of the railings, indicating that the street level in this area was raised substantially at some stage.

With Thanks to The Calico Basket

Alison Brown 1994.

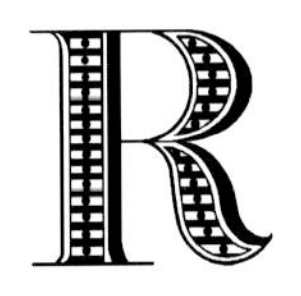

Name and Address	*Telephone*

St. Malachi's Parish Church

A church was built on this site in 1662 by Colonel Arthur Hill. Dripstones survive from this building and are fixed beneath the windows. Between 1760 and 1772 the church was rebuilt by Wills Hill, first Marquis of Downshire, at a cost of £20,000. He intended that it should become a cathedral and the Bishop's Throne, which still exists, is a reminder of this unfulfilled dream. Visitors will notice the high oak box pews, designed for warmth in the days before central heating. There are two organs, one built by a Bavarian, John Snetzler, and the other by his pupil, George Pike England. The tower and spire rise to a height of 210 feet and house a peal of 10 bells.

Alison Brown 1994.

Name and Address	*Telephone*

ARTHUR STREET

When it was first built Arthur Street was called 'New Street' before acquiring its present name in honour of Lord Arthur Hill. The tudor-style cottages were built in 1850 for workers and tenants of the Downshire Estate. One of the houses which faces on to Ballynahinch Street was a blacksmith's shop, but it lost its roof after lying derelict for a number of years. At the end of the street is a blocked brick archway, indicating that there was once access to the 'Pleasure Ground' behind.

With Thanks to E. P. Patterson

SEXTON
Alison Brown 1994.

Name and Address	*Telephone*

The Gatelodges

The gatelodges at the foot of the church avenue were erected in 1772 to provide schoolhouses for the local children. The left hand lodge (illustrated here) was the girls' schoolroom, whilst the right one was for boys. The pupils were known as the 'Bluecoat Children' on account of the colour of their uniform. Both schools ceased to be used in 1887 when a new school was opened in Ballynahinch Street. In 1910 the girls' school was refurbished for use as the Sexton's House, replacing 'Rose Cottage' which stood half-way between the church and the road. The boys' school became a hall.

With Thanks to the Red Fox Coffee Shop

Alison Brown 1994.

Name and Address	*Telephone*

The Chapel of Cromlyn

Although there has been an ecclesiastical foundation in this area since about 600 AD, the Chapel of Cromlyn was dedicated to St. Malachi who lived in the twelfth century. He was called Malachi O'Morgair and was the Bishop of Down and Archbishop of Armagh. The 1622 Ulster Visitation describes the chapel as 'being in ruins' and it was not until 1636 that a new place of worship was provided. The rough doorway which can be seen today is probably not a true remnant of the chapel, but is merely a Georgian garden ornament built with the remaining stones.

With Thanks to the White Gables Hotel

Alison Brown.

Name and Address	*Telephone*

NUMBER 9, MAIN STREET

This house has perhaps one of the best Georgian doorcases in the whole town, having been built towards the end of the eighteenth century when the town was being greatly expanded. It is approached up a flight of five steps and sports an attractive fanlight with radiating glazing bars. This design is very sophisticated for a rural town and reflects the architecture which the builder, the First Marquis of Downshire, would have seen in London. No. 11, next door has a similar, but less elaborate doorcase.

With Thanks to Cornerstone

Alison Brown 1994

Name and Address	*Telephone*

STONE HOUSES, 23-27 MAIN STREET

Little remains of seventeenth century architecture in Hillsborough, but these stone houses would have been built at that time and then renovated during the eighteenth century as part of the reconstruction of the street. At one stage during its history No. 23 was a shop and the shop front remained in place until the early 1980's when the building was extensively refurbished and saved from dereliction. At one time these houses would probably have been thatched and their position shows how little the original line of Main Street has moved in over 300 years.

With Thanks to N.I. Textiles Assoc./The Irish Linen Guild

Alison Brown 1994.

Name and Address	*Telephone*

THE LAKE

The area now covered by the lake was once an avenue of trees leading to the house where the Downshire family lived. In her diary, Mrs Delaney, the wife of the Dean of Down, describes the area and how Wills Hill intended to build a new house for his family and give the other to the Bishop of Down. This would have furthered his aim of making Hillsborough Parish Church a cathedral. However when he began building his new house, Hillsborough Castle, the old house was demolished, and the lake created on the site. There are races which feed from this lake through to the lake in the grounds of the Castle providing the pleasant ornamental streams in the gardens.

With Thanks to Pik-Kwik

Alison Brown 1994

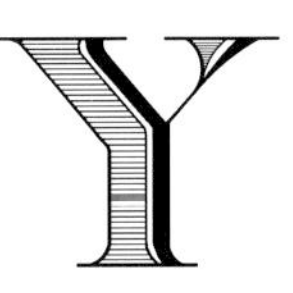

Name and Address	*Telephone*

THE COUNCIL OFFICES

The imposing offices of Lisburn Borough Council stand on the south side of the Square. This building was erected in 1964 for the now defunct Hillsborough Rural District Council and was designed in Georgian style to complement the architecture of the area. Until 1943 this was the site of the Royal Corporation Arms Hotel which had been in operation since the 18th century. The hotel had to be demolished after being gutted by fire in that year. Like the Council Offices, the hotel was a red brick building, but it stood closer to the street, giving the Square a greater sense of enclosure.

With Thanks to Lisburn Borough Council

Alison Brown 1994.

Name and Address	*Telephone*

Lady Alice's Temple

In 1895 the 'Yew Walk' was created in the grounds of Hillsborough Castle on the site of the old Moira Road which ran off the town square. At the end of this walk, above a pool, stands Lady Alice's Temple which was named after the sister of Lord Arthur Hill. This is a classical style structure in the form of a rotunda. The temple acts as an 'eye-catcher' at the end of an avenue of lime trees. These limes line a broad avenue carpeted in delicate moss. The creation of this part of the gardens was the last work the Hills carried out on the castle and its grounds before selling the property.

With Thanks to Andrew of Hillsborough Ltd.

Local Business and Service Directory

Today Hillsborough is a town renowned not only for its beautiful architecture, but also for its high class shopping and established service industries.

We would like to thank the following businesses without whose help and support this book would not have been possible.

Unless otherwise stated all businesses listed are in Hillsborough (STD code 0846)

	Tel	Fax
Auctioneers		
BOWERS AUCTIONEERS		
THE SHAMBLES, DROMORE ROAD	683840	689528
Bank		
NORTHERN BANK LIMITED		
20 BALLYNAHINCH STREET	682217	
Chemist		
V.E. REANEY CHEMIST		
12 LISBURN STREET	682207	682207
Clothing For All Seasons Outdoors		
THE OUTDOOR CLOTHING COMPANY		
13 LISBURN STREET	689496	683138
Coffee Merchant		
JOHNSON BROTHERS (BELFAST) LTD		
137 HILLSBOROUGH OLD ROAD, LISBURN	679121	668800
Coffee Shop		
RED FOX COFFEE SHOP		
6 MAIN STREET	682586	
Craft Shop		
P. R. COWDY CRAFTS		
20 MAIN STREET	682455	
Estate Agent		
CORNERSTONE		
2 LISBURN STREET	682873/683103	
Gallery		
THE CHATHAM CHEST GALLERY & SHIPPRINT PUBLISHING		
21 LISBURN STREET	689165	(0232) 640481
Hotel		
WHITE GABLES HOTEL		
14 DROMORE ROAD	682755	689532
Insurance Brokers		
G & H BELL LTD.		
2A LISBURN STREET	683104	682174

	Tel	Fax
Ladies Fashions		
THE OLD COACH HOUSE		
THE MEWS, 12 MAIN STREET	682521	
Local Government		
LISBURN BOROUGH COUNCIL		
THE SQUARE	682477	689016
Newsagent		
PIK –KWIK		
7 BALLYNAHINCH STREET	683315	
Patchwork & Quilting Supply Store		
THE CALICO BASKET		
6A MAIN STREET	682863	
Painting and Decorating		
DOWN DECORATORS		
10 LISBURN STREET	682684	689521
Pharmacy		
E. P. PATTERSON		
7 LISBURN STREET	682963	
Portrait Studio		
THE DAVID GRAHAM STUDIO		
14 MAIN STREET	683335	683751
Restaurant & Bar		
THE HILLSIDE		
21–23 MAIN STREET	682765	682557
Specialist Suppliers to the Food Industry		
ANDREW OF HILLSBOROUGH LTD.		
141 DROMORE ROAD	683030	683798
Trade Association		
NORTHERN IRELAND TEXTILES ASSOC./THE IRISH LINEN GUILD		
5C THE SQUARE	689999	689968
Yarn Merchants		
JOHN PRESTON AND CO. (BELFAST) LTD.		
29 – 31 LISBURN STREET	682671	689584

Open Diary

This section is provided to record personal dates such as birthdays, anniversaries and other important annual events.

January

1

2

3

4

5

6

7

8

9

10

11

12

13

14

15

16

17

18

19

20

21

22

23

24

25

26

27

28

29

30

31

February

1

2

3

4

5

6

7

8

9

10

11

12

13

14

15

16

17

18

19

20

21

22

23

24

25

26

27

28

29

March

1

2

3

4

5

6

7

8

9

10

11

12

13

14

15

16

17

18

19

20

21

22

23

24

25

26

27

28

29

30

31

April

1

2

3

4

5

6

7

8

9

10

11

12

13

14

15

16

17

18

19

20

21

22

23

24

25

26

27

28

29

30

May

1

2

3

4

5

6

7

8

9

10

11

12

13

14

15

16

17

18

19

20

21

22

23

24

25

26

27

28

29

30

31

June

1

2

3

4

5

6

7

8

9

10

11

12

13

14

15

16

17

18

19

20

21

22

23

24

25

26

27

28

29

30

July

1

2

3

4

5

6

7

8

9

10

11

12

13

14

15

16

17

18

19

20

21

22

23

24

25

26

27

28

29

30

31

August

1

2

3

4

5

6

7

8

9

10

11

12

13

14

15

16

17

18

19

20

21

22

23

24

25

26

27

28

29

30

31

September

1

2

3

4

5

6

7

8

9

10

11

12

13

14

15

16

17

18

19

20

21

22

23

24

25

26

27

28

29

30

October

1

2

3

4

5

6

7

8

9

10

11

12

13

14

15

16

17

18

19

20

21

22

23

24

25

26

27

28

29

30

31

November

1

2

3

4

5

6

7

8

9

10

11

12

13

14

15

16

17

18

19

20

21

22

23

24

25

26

27

28

29

30

December

1

2

3

4

5

6

7

8

9

10

11

12

13

14

15

16

17

18

19

20

21

22

23

24

25

26

27

28

29

30

31

Dear Reader

We hope you have found this book both enjoyable and useful. If you feel that it could have been improved in any way do please let us know.

This book is one of our 'Illustrated History and Companion' series. Other towns and areas currently featured in this range include:–

Ballycastle and the Heart of the Glens
Ballymena
Bangor
Donaghadee
Holywood
Newtownards

If you require more information call us on 0247 883876 or write to:–

Cottage Publications
15 Ballyhay Road
Donaghadee
Co. Down
N. Ireland
BT21 0NG

Timothy S Johnston